5 SECONDS OF SUMMER

THE ULTIMATE FAN BOOK

Malcolm Croft

BARRON'S

First edition for North America published in 2014
by Barron's Educational Series, Inc.

All inquiries should be addressed to:
Barron's Educational Series, Inc.
250 Wireless Boulevard
Hauppauge, New York 11788
www.barronseduc.com

ISBN: 978-0-7641-6761-4

Library of Congress Control Number: 2014941228

Date of Manufacture: July 2014
Manufactured by: Oriental Press, Dubai, UAE

Printed in Dubai, UAE

9 8 7 6 5 4 3 2 1

CONTENTS

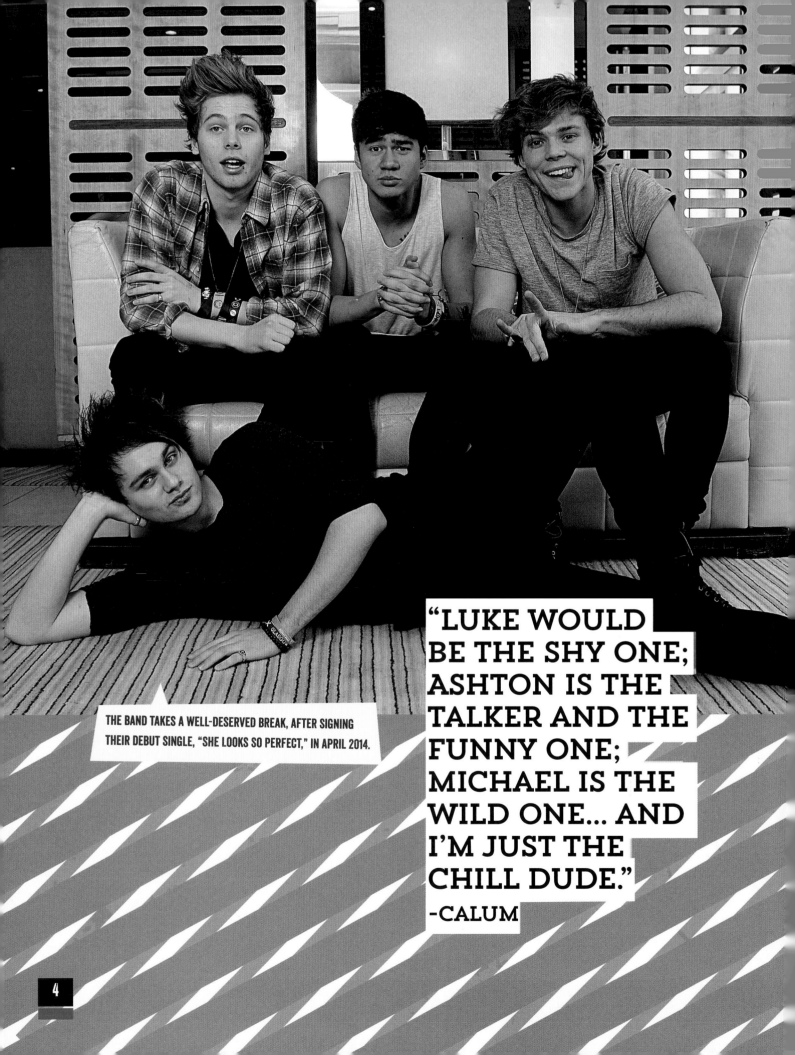

THE BAND TAKES A WELL-DESERVED BREAK, AFTER SIGNING THEIR DEBUT SINGLE, "SHE LOOKS SO PERFECT," IN APRIL 2014.

"LUKE WOULD BE THE SHY ONE; ASHTON IS THE TALKER AND THE FUNNY ONE; MICHAEL IS THE WILD ONE... AND I'M JUST THE CHILL DUDE."
-CALUM

SUMMER TIME!

5 Seconds of Summer are, without a doubt, the world's hottest band.

From the very second their debut single "Out of My Limit" catapulted them from YouTube stars to rock gods — with over 3.5 million views in under a week — the world knew in a heartbeat that a new pop phenomenon had been born. With Luke's beautiful blue eyes and rock 'n' roll lip piercing — a punk Harry Styles? — to Michael's one-of-a-kind "reverse skunk" trademark hairstyle, 5SOS are much more than just the "new One Direction." They are unique. They are themselves. They write their own songs, play their own instruments, and style their own hair. They even created their own record label before they released their own debut album. And they are here to rock your socks off!

They are also the very best of friends, brothers from other mothers, a tight-knit gang of musicians with a vision and an obvious chemistry that any fan can see. This four-piece band from Australia is not just your average boy band with a five-second shelf life — it is here to stay. You think you know them now? You haven't seen anything yet!

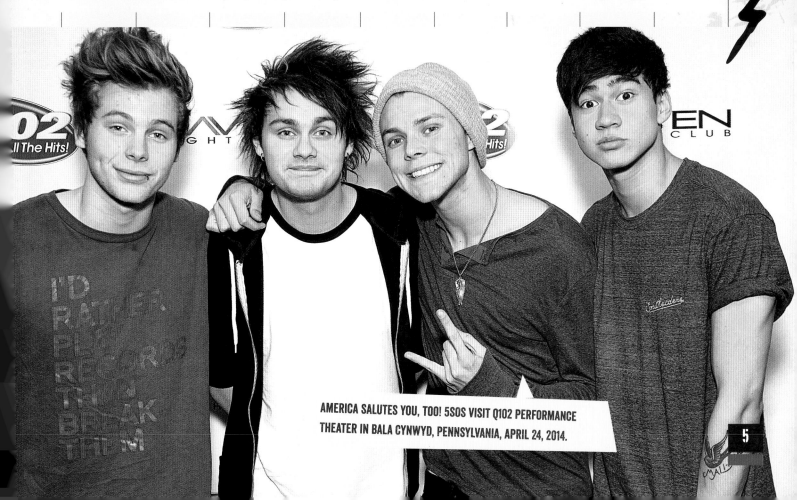

AMERICA SALUTES YOU, TOO! 5SOS VISIT Q102 PERFORMANCE THEATER IN BALA CYNWYD, PENNSYLVANIA, APRIL 24, 2014.

LUKE

THE GROUP'S PARTY-LOVING LEAD VOCALIST AND GUITARIST HAS TRAVELED ALL THE WAY FROM RIVERSTONE, SYDNEY, AUSTRALIA TO ENTERTAIN THE WORLD WITH HIS STRAIGHT-UP ATTITUDE ... AND HAIR!

LUKE PLAYING ONE OF HIS FIRST CONCERTS — AT SCHOOL, AGE 14!

"Hey I'm Luke and I like to party!" This is Luke's introduction to the world on Instagram, the social media network that the teenage lead singer and guitarist of the world's hottest new pop-punk boy band has nearly broken in two, thanks to the influx of his rapidly growing, and incredibly devoted, fanbase — two million followers and counting!

Since 2011, Luke — with his Instagram username "luke_is_a_penguin" (his favorite animal, if you didn't know already!) — has been reaching out to his fans from the very second he felt comfortable singing and playing guitar at the same time. The talented singer has been posting videos and images to Twitter, Facebook, and, of course, YouTube since he was just 14 years old. In three short years, Luke has posted over 6,000 hilarious tweets and images (that's over five a day!) directly to his fans — proof that Luke likes to tell his fans what he's up to, including what's he's having for dinner and breakfast!

Luke, the tallest, youngest ("but most responsible," so he says!), member of the band, cites his bad habits as "procrastinating" and "banding" as well as "constantly making a mess in the shower — it's like a tsunami!" The rest of the band dread sharing a hotel room with the lead singer.

"We weren't really friends with Calum at school because I didn't think I was cool enough to be his friend," Luke once said, though it's hard to imagine Luke not being cool, isn't it?

This blond, guitar playing heartthrob with a big heart has a reputation for being a jokester. He goofs off in front of the camera, answers interview questions as humorously as possible, and makes fun of his bandmates 24 hours a day — you should check out their scores of hilarious twitcam videos online!

"IT DOESN'T FEEL LIKE THREE YEARS HAS GONE BY; IT FEELS MORE LIKE TEN."

LUKE

5 SOS STATS!

Born: July 16, 1996
Favorite color: Blue
Pet: A dog named Molly
Perfect date: Day on beach, then ice cream!
Favorite food: Chicken

LUKE SENDS HIS FANS INTO A PUNK-POP MELTDOWN AT LONDON'S SHEPHERDS BUSH EMPIRE IN MARCH 2014.

16-YEAR-OLD CALUM ROCKS THE ASSEMBLY AT NORWEST CHRISTIAN COLLEGE.

5 SOS STATS!

Born: January 25, 1996

Siblings: Mali Koa, sister

Favorite color: Blue

Favorite movie: Monsters, Inc.

Favorite food: Pasta and pizza (ham and pineapple)

CALUM TREATS HIS FANS AT TORONTO'S SOUND ACADEMY IN APRIL 2014.

CALUM

///

*THE BAND'S RESIDENT BASSIST AND SONGWRITER IS THE QUIETEST MEMBER ...
OR AT LEAST HE WOULD WANT YOU TO THINK SO! THIS OUTGOING GUY IS IN FACT
THE OWNER OF THE BAND MEMBER WITH THE SHARPEST WIT, AS WELL AS THE
PROUD OWNER OF THE MOST OUTRAGEOUS UNDERWEAR.*

"**C**alum is the weirdest person in the band, but he refuses to admit it," Michael teases in a recent interview. But he's allowed to, as he has been Calum's closest friend since high school. "He also has a good bum for mooning!" he continues. The rest of the guys agree. And Calum is more than happy to show off his bottom to his fans, as many photos on Twitter and Instagram demonstrate! When he's not putting himself on display, the bass player is known for owning the band's strangest underwear.

"I don't know about you guys but I always seem to have toucans on my underwear!" he famously once joked. "I've always got animals on my underwear. It's embarrassing!"

Michael still teases Calum about the band's early days: "I don't know how it happened that Calum got in the band. No one officially asked Calum to join! He was just friends with us and assumed he was in the band."

In those days, before those first band practices at Michael's parents' house, the band's success — and even friendship — wasn't so assured. "At first, Michael didn't like Luke," Calum states. "And I was best friends with Michael I had no choice but to not like Luke either, but in the back of my mind I was like, 'but Luke seems like a really cool guy!'"

The boys' love of loud punk rock while growing up in a sleepy and quiet surburban town is what brought these four unique individuals and personalities together. They wanted to wake up the neighborhood!

And the guys like to think that because they didn't like each other at first, but now do, it should hold them in good stead for the future, especially when years of touring, fame, money, and fighting often can tear bands apart. The guys often joke that because they started off hating each other, they got it out of the way early. The future should be smooth sailing then...

CALUM TRIES TO GET HIS BANDMATES TO LAUGH WHILE LIVE ON AIR ON THE *ELVIS DURAN* SHOW!

MICHAEL

THE BAND'S BLEACHED BLOND, AND PINK, AND PURPLE, AND BLUE, GUITARIST'S HAIRSTYLE IS KNOWN AS THE "REVERSE SKUNK," SO IT'S NO WONDER MICHAEL IS THE "WILD ONE" OF THE GROUP (SAYS CALUM!), BUT HE'S ALSO THE MOST HONEST ABOUT BEING TAKEN SERIOUSLY AS A MUSICIAN AND SONGWRITER...

"I literally can't remember *not* being in a band, I can't remember anything before December 3, 2011!" Michael exclaimed in an online interview, still pinching himself that his wildest dreams have come true. As a renowned gamer and loud talker, Michael can often be found — when not on stage that is — lying in bed and playing computer games. In fact, both Luke and Michael almost didn't allow Ashton in the band because he didn't like playing FIFA on the PS2!

It was Michael who first had the idea to form a band, and it was Michael's parents' house that bore the brunt of loud and unrehearsed teenage noises during the very first band practices. "I saw Luke's videos on YouTube and they were getting really popular, and I thought 'I should get in on this!'" Michael joked in 2012, recalling the moment he knew that being in a band was his claim to fame.

In many of the band's hilarious interviews on-line, it is Michael who often plays the clown, answering questions in as silly a way as possible and sticking his tongue out, but he is also responsible for the boys' most sensitive moments, too: "It was a dream of ours to be up on a stage playing our own original music and to have crowds sing our songs back at us! At our first show in Sydney that happened, and it was the most amazing thing ever. From then on, as a band, we have been working as hard as we can; I guess you could say the 'band' dream gets bigger every day as we are always setting more and more goals for us."

In March 2014, Michael sent the world's music press into a frenzy. He revealed to *MTV News* the moment he saw Harry Styles naked! "All I remember is Harry coming in to our room," Michael teased, "stealing all our fruit, throwing fruit at us, tipping our tables over, and then running away naked. It was traumatizing." Thankfully, Harry didn't mind Michael revealing all — 5SOS was asked to tour again with One Direction in June 2014. Phew!

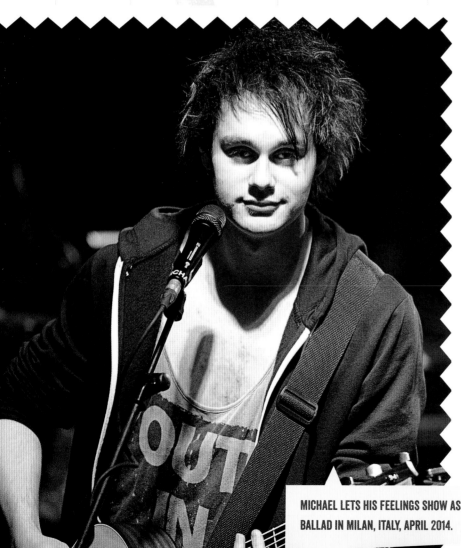

MICHAEL LETS HIS FEELINGS SHOW AS HE PLAYS A SLOW ACOUSTIC BALLAD IN MILAN, ITALY, APRIL 2014.

5 SOS STATS! ⚡

Born: November 20, 1995

Middle name: Gordon (he hates it!)

Favorite color: Green

Favorite movie: Forrest Gump

Favorite chocolate: Cadbury's Twirl

MICHAEL CAN'T QUITE BELIEVE HOW AMAZING HIS FANS ARE AT THE BEST BUY THEATER, NEW YORK, APRIL 22, 2014.

THE "REVERSE SKUNK" IN ALL ITS FULL GLORY — COMPLETE WITH MICHAEL'S ALWAYS ON-SHOW TONGUE! IN MANCHESTER, APRIL 2014.

ASHTON

//

DESPITE BEING THE LAST TO JOIN THE BAND, IN DECEMBER 2011, DRUMMER ASHTON IS ACTUALLY THE OLDEST. TWO YEARS OLDER THAN THE BAND'S BABY, LUKE, YOU WOULD THINK ASHTON WOULD BE THE WISEST. BUT NO! HE IS ACTUALLY THE SILLIEST MEMBER OF THE BAND.

PLEASE DO NOT OPEN THIS DOOR!!!!

Beat-keeper Ashton — who the rest of the guys claim has the worst bad habit of the band ("Let's just say he's messy at toenail clipping") is still one of the nicest guys in music! From the very earliest band rehearsals, Ashton has been the glue that has kept the band not only in time, but together. Ashton was the missing piece of the puzzle. Luke, Michael, and Calum spent six months uploading covers up to YouTube before Ashton — or Ash, as he is known — joined the gang. And the foursome have been inseparable since that day. "We haven't stopped since day one," Ashton recalls. "We've spent every waking hour getting to where we are now." Ashton was a friend of a friend of a friend who got in touch with Michael when he heard they were looking for a drummer for a gig, though their paths had crossed before this point. "I first met Luke at the movies," Ashton remembers in an online interview. "He was getting teased for these fluoro-green glasses he was wearing. I went up to him and said 'I kind of like your glasses ... they look cool". Many people believe that Ashton and Luke are twins because of their looks, with Ashton and Luke getting the majority of the girls' attention ... so far! "We are still surprised that girls like our band," says Ashton. "We're very lucky people want photos with us because we know one day they won't." Not any day soon Ashton, don't you worry!

'1, 2, 3, 4!' ASHTON CALLS OUT AT THE PALAIS THEATRE, MELBOURNE, ON MAY 3, 2014. THE FANS RESPONDED IN UNISON WITH "5, S, O, S!"

A SPECTACULAR "NO PLACE LIKE HOME" SHOW AT THE ENMORE THEATRE IN SYDNEY, APRIL 30, 2014.

5 SOS STATS! ⚡

Born: July 7, 1996

Middle name: Fletcher

Favorite color: Blue

Favorite food: Spaghetti

Other instruments: Saxophone, piano, and guitar

ASHTON, OR ASH AS THE BAND CALL HIM, POUNDS THE SKINS OF HIS CUSTOM-MADE DRUM KIT, APRIL 2014.

NEW DIRECTION

INSPIRED BY THEIR LOVE OF AMERICAN PUNK-POP BANDS BLINK 182, YELLOWCARD, AND GREEN DAY — AS WELL AS AUSTRALIAN BAND AMY MEREDITH — LUKE HEMMINGS, CALUM HOOD, AND MICHAEL CLIFFORD FORMED 5SOS, "OFFICIALLY," ON APRIL 3, 2011. ASHTON, LIKE MOST DRUMMERS, ARRIVED LATER THAN THE OTHER MEMBERS, BUT THE BAND'S FATE, AND FUTURE, WAS SEALED DURING A MATH LESSON AT NORWEST CHRISTIAN COLLEGE WHEN THE BOYS FINALLY DECIDED ON THEIR BAND NAME...

5 Seconds of Summer was formed, strangely, in Australia's winter. While the band's name is a supposed spoof of the popular, but offbeat, 2009 romantic comedy, *500 Days of Summer*, in a recent interview, the comedic clown of the band, guitarist Michael, said that if the band were a girl band they'd probably be called "The Powerpuff Blokes," though we're not sure what the rest of the band would think about that! And while the fledgling group from Sydney's suburbs were initially tempted to audition for the Australian version of *The X Factor* (if only to meet Danni Minogue!), the boys took a group vote and instead decided against it — they didn't want to become known as "that band from the *X Factor.*" They didn't want to end up as a "manufactured"

A VERY EARLY PHOTOSHOOT FOR THE BAND, IN SYDNEY, 2012. LOOK AT THOSE HAIRSTYLES!

group with no control over their music. It has been 5SOS's manifesto right from their very first band rehearsal to be as authentic as possible — because that is exactly what they are — "real people." "I guess we always wanted to be a rock band," Ashton said in an early interview. "We always looked up to bands like Green Day, and it was really important to us to stand up for what we wanted to do as a band."

"MAYBE WE SHOULD START A BAND?"
MICHAEL

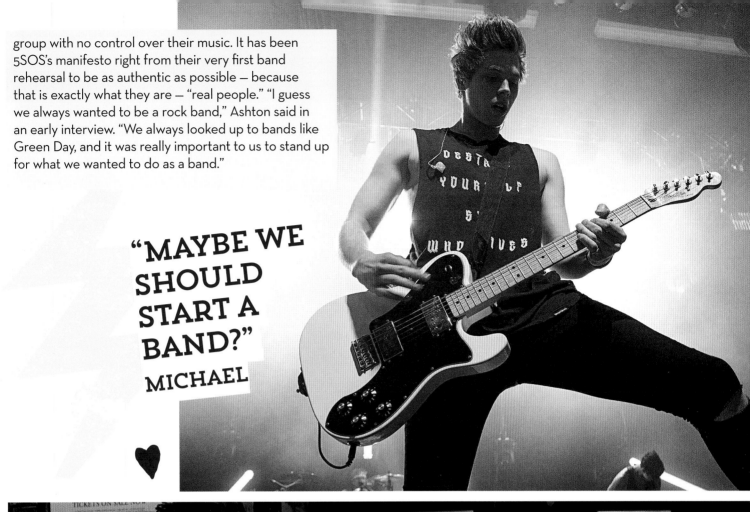

YOUNG AND HOPEFUL: THE BOYS AT AN EARLY PHOTOSHOOT IN SYDNEY IN 2012.

SCHOOL'S OUT

SCHOOL PLAYED AN INTEGRAL PART IN THE FORMATION OF THE BAND. THEY EVEN DREAMT UP THE NAME DURING A MATH LESSON!

The sleepy suburb of Riverstone, in the state of New South Wales (on the eastern side of Australia), isn't just the home of each of the members of 5SOS, it is also the very birthplace of the band itself — Norwest Christian College. The college is where the four band members first met, as juniors, and played their earliest shows to their friends and other students. They are now the college's most famous alumni, for sure!

One of the school's goals is "that each child in our care learns to maintain a vibrant inner life full of hope and optimism driven by their own sense of purpose." That sounds just like 5SOS's guide to living life, don't you think?

Though the band's teenage years were eternally sunny (it's Australia after all!), the boys' formative years as future best friends didn't always look so bright.

"I remember in freshman year, Luke and I hated each other," Michael remembers, smiling. "He wanted to kill me and I wanted to kill him and then somehow ... we became best friends." The guitarists later recalled it was their love of guitars and learning to play the chords to Blink 182's song, "I Miss You," their favorite song, that bonded them together forever.

"In 2011 I was working in a video shop and Luke had quit school," Ashton recalls. "I was a drummer in the local area and these boys needed a drummer for their first gig, so I went and played with them and it just felt really right on stage ... and so I joined the band that day." Luke recalls later that only 12 people showed up to that historic gig in December 2011! After the show, to say "thank you" to Ashton for helping the guys out when they needed a drummer at the last minute, Calum got "down on one knee and proposed to Ashton to be in the band." ("There's a photo of this moment," Luke reckons!) Ashton said "yes" ... and the rest is becoming record-breaking history!

AN EARLY BREAKOUT GIG — HYDE PARK, SYDNEY, AUGUST 2012.

CALUM AND MICHAEL ONSTAGE
PERFORMING TOGETHER, AGE 15!

17

BLINK 182, A 5SOS FAVE BAND AND WRITERS OF "I MISS YOU," AN EARLY YOUTUBE VID FOR 5SOS.

BILLY JOE AND TRÉ COOL OF PUNK BAND GREEN DAY — ONE OF 5SOS'S BIGGEST MUSICAL AND FASHION INFLUENCES.

UNDER THE INFLUENCE

THE BAND WEARS THEIR MUSICAL INSPIRATION PROUDLY — AND OFTEN LITERALLY — ON THEIR T-SHIRT SLEEVES; AT THEIR LIVE SHOWS THEY CAN USUALLY BE SEEN WEARING RAMONES, NIRVANA, OR GREEN DAY T-SHIRTS — USUALLY RIPPED! IN THEIR EARLY DAYS, THE BAND BONDED OVER THEIR SHARED LOVE OF BLINK 182, THEIR FAVORITE GROUP, BUT THERE WERE MANY OTHER ARTISTS WHO HELPED SHAPE THE YOUNG 5SOS INTO ROCK GODS OF THE FUTURE.

Luke's first CD was American punk band Good Charlotte's *The Young and the Helpless* album, and you can hear its heavy influence in many of 5SOS's punkiest songs. But in tracks like "Heartache on the Big Screen" and "Out of My Limit," the boys' love of catchy singalong pop shines through, too — and this comes from the band's natural gift for writing well-crafted melodies. "Our influences are pop punk and rock bands," Michael told the world in 2013, "bands like McFly, Blink 182, Green Day, Busted, All Time Low, Boys Like Girls. We all like lots of music and have been listening to a lot of different stuff since we were young." This fusion of influences, of heavier punk bands with more pop boy bands, has given this band a unique place in their fans' and music critics' hearts — there is currently no "boy band" on the planet that rocks as hard as 5SOS!

POPULAR AUSTRALIAN ROCK BAND, AMY MEREDITH. A HUGE INFLUENCE ON THE 5SOS SOUND.

"WE AREN'T A BOY BAND." LUKE

WEARING THEIR INFLUENCES ON THEIR SLEEVES — WITH RIPPED BLACK JEANS AND T-SHIRTS — 5SOS DON'T LOOK LIKE A TRADITIONAL BOY BAND, DO THEY?

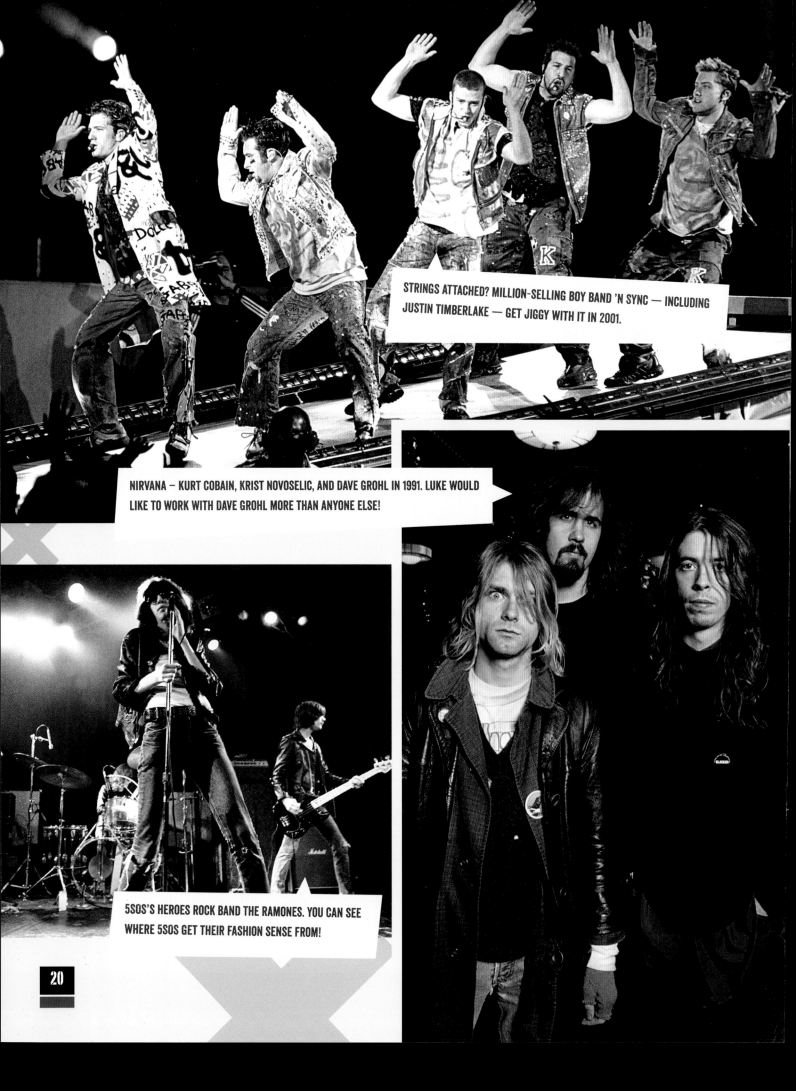

STRINGS ATTACHED? MILLION-SELLING BOY BAND 'N SYNC — INCLUDING JUSTIN TIMBERLAKE — GET JIGGY WITH IT IN 2001.

NIRVANA — KURT COBAIN, KRIST NOVOSELIC, AND DAVE GROHL IN 1991. LUKE WOULD LIKE TO WORK WITH DAVE GROHL MORE THAN ANYONE ELSE!

5SOS'S HEROES ROCK BAND THE RAMONES. YOU CAN SEE WHERE 5SOS GET THEIR FASHION SENSE FROM!

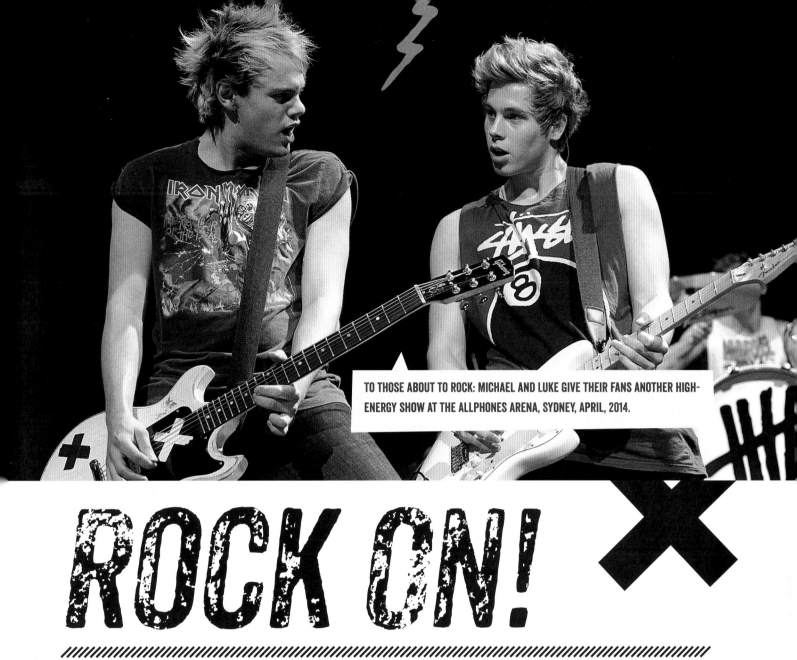

TO THOSE ABOUT TO ROCK: MICHAEL AND LUKE GIVE THEIR FANS ANOTHER HIGH-ENERGY SHOW AT THE ALLPHONES ARENA, SYDNEY, APRIL, 2014.

ROCK ON!

While many of their critics may call 5SOS a "boy band" (they are boys in a band, for sure!), these boys definitely aren't your typical pop stars. Their songs have a more rock 'n' roll edge than most of their contempories and the band was not "manufactured" artificially either. They formed the band by themselves, play their own instruments, write their own songs, rehearsed every day until their fingers and thumbs hurt, booked their own gigs, promoted themselves on social media — they are homegrown. They are not just four separate guys who play music ... they are a *band*, and proud! "We're heavily influenced by '90s pop punk bands like Green Day, Good Charlotte, and Yellowcard," Calum stated in a 2013 interview. "So, what we want to do is kind of modernize that and bring back the whole band thing."

"Boy bands" of today are no longer the squeaky-clean-cheesy-dance-routine acts of the past 20 years.

5 Seconds of Summer is the first of a new breed of "boy band." They play their own instruments, speak their mind, are allowed relationships with girlfriends (once a big no-no, as band managers also thought it alienated young female fans!), and are allowed to express themselves however they choose, whenever they choose.

It wasn't always like that: social networking sites such as Twitter, Instagram, and Facebook have been instrumental in creating boy bands where the fans can hear what their favorite band members have to say, when they say it. It has served to show those people in the music industry that what the fans want is not a factory line of identical personalities in a band that plays other people's songs — they want their favorite bands and band members to relate to them personally and let the fans into their world! Bands like One Direction and, now, 5 Seconds of Summer have changed the music industry for the better, forever!

TAKE-OFF!

AS THE BAND EXPLODES INTO THE GLOBAL POP STRATOSPHERE, WITH NO LIMITS HOLDING THEM BACK, 5SOS HAVE RETAINED MUCH CONTROL OVER THEIR OWN FUTURE BY CONQUERING THE MUSIC INDUSTRY ALL BY THEMSELVES. NOT BAD FOR A GROUP OF MUSICIANS WHO FLUNKED MUSIC CLASSES AT SCHOOL.

"I went to TAFE for music, a course for arts, media, and entertainment in NSW, and I failed music performance. It was a pretty sad moment really!" Ashton admitted, rolling around laughing, in a 2014 interview. Michael didn't do much better: "I got a D in music!" he beamed proudly about this underachievement. When it comes to being A-star pupils, Calum and Luke are the group's top dogs. "I got an A in music," Luke announced, while Calum attained "a B or a C" (he couldn't remember at the time!). "Me and Calum are holding it together with our A's and B's," joked Luke. "5SOS's average grade in music is a C!" Ashton quipped. But when you're in 5SOS, music isn't about the rules and grades. It's about the rock and roll spirit of the music.

When the band released their *Somewhere New* EP in December 2012, six months after they put out their *Unplugged* EP (when apparently the entire band was

THE BAND FINALLY GET WHAT THEY DESERVE — THEIR NAME IN LIGHTS! A SELL-OUT SHOW FROM THE FIRST HEADLINE TOUR IN THE USA.

THE BAND VISIT THE "ELVIS DURAN Z100 MORNING SHOW" AT Z100 STUDIO ON APRIL 24, 2014 IN NEW YORK CITY.

ill, but decided to record it anyway), their growing fanbase went crazy over their homegrown, self-penned songs "Out of My Limit" and "Unpredictable." But it is with the release of their songs online, such as "The Only Reason" and "Heartache On The Big Screen" that saw the band take off, and gain respect from not only their fans, but their critics, too. "Giving songs away to the fans," as Luke called it, is what 5SOS's early success was all about. Building a fanbase came first; this was more important to the band than trying to secure a record deal or appear on TV. This fresh way of thinking is what sets the young band apart from many other modern artists who are hungry for fame. Their approach is also inspiring lots of other songwriters in their bedrooms — just like Luke, Calum, Michael, and Ashton — to do the same. 5SOS are starting a revolution! And it's this DIY approach to the music industry that will keep the band grounded, as they launch themselves as serious artists who just want their music to be heard.

"I think it's down to where we grew up and how we grew up, too," Michael stated in a interview about how important it is to remain as grounded as mass-superstardom beckons. "It wasn't like we were that privileged. We learned to appreciate everything and everyone around us. And when we started the band, that feeling never really left us." Ashton agrees; "The one thing you always need to remember is that you don't know everything, nobody does in this industry, and you learn new things every day. That keeps us grounded. The one thing I love about being in this band is that I don't think we hide anything at all. If we mess up, we mess up, we're just real people."

THE STAGE CAN NO LONGER CONTAIN LUKE AS HE TAKES OFF. THE BAND'S ENERGETIC SHOWS ARE ALREADY FAMOUS.

WE HAVE TAKE-OFF! 5SOS ARE NO LONGER JUST FOUR ORDINARY TEENAGE BOYS FROM RIVERSTONE, SYDNEY. THEY ARE NOW SUPERSTARS.

THE BAND'S FANS SHOW THEIR SUPPORT, AND A SELECTION OF 5SOS MERCHANDISE ITEMS, AT THE PALAIS THEATRE, MELBOURNE, AUSTRALIA, MAY 3, 2014.

LUKE AND CALUM ARE ALWAYS SWAPPING NOTES, LICKS, RIFFS, AND FUNNY FACES!

PHONES GALORE: FANS UPLOAD THEIR OWN 5SOS VIDEOS DURING A PERFORMANCE IN SYDNEY.

NO LIMITS

THE BAND'S DIY APPROACH TO CREATING MUSIC AND PROMOTING THEMSELVES TIRELESSLY WITH ONLY THE HELP OF THEIR FANS IS WHAT HAS SET THEM APART FROM EVERY OTHER NEW BAND. THE BOYS' EXHAUSTIVE DEDICATION TO SOCIAL MEDIA HAS HELPED THEM BUILD A LOYAL FANBASE OF MILLIONS OF DEVOTED BOYS AND GIRLS BEFORE THEY BEGAN THEIR CAREER. THIS IS THE KEY TO THEIR VERY UNIQUE SUCCESS.

When Luke, just 14, posted videos of himself playing covers of Justin Bieber's songs on YouTube, he never expected to actually get any views. "I put some videos up on YouTube of myself singing and playing really badly!" he said, modest as ever. These videos started becoming popular with hometown friends and schoolmates from Norwest Christian College, and word started to quickly spread online of the teenager's talent. It wasn't long before Michael, Luke, and Calum were uploading acoustic covers with Luke, and writing songs together.

Over the next year, the band played local shows together, joined Twitter and Facebook and started a social media campaign that is still blowing the doors wide open for them, as well as seeing them become nominated for the Shorty Awards 2014 — the glitzy, and prestigious, honor that awards the "best use of social media." They lost out to girl band Fifth Harmony.

"It would be much harder to share with our fans without Facebook and Twitter, for sure," Luke says. "I think fans have changed and how they support musicians has changed. People want to know about you and who you are; without the ways to speak to them, I really don't think we would be where we are today." Ashton agrees: "Social media for us has been huge for connecting with the fans. It's also been important for us to make sure our fans know exactly who we are, where we are, and what we're doing."

If you haven't started following the band on Twitter and Instragram, then what are you waiting for? Each band member has millions of followers already!

INSTAGRAM
LUKEISAPENGUIN
MICHAELGCLIFFORD
CALUMHOOD
ASHTONIRWIN

TWITTER
@LUKE5SOS
@MICHAEL5SOS
@CALUM5SOS
@ASHTON5SOS

5SOS PERFORM AT THE SOUND ACADEMY, TORONTO, APRIL, 2014, ON THEIR FIRST NORTH AMERICAN TOUR.

ONE FOR THE RADIO

5SOS DON'T JUST PLAY THEIR OWN INSTRUMENTS. THEY WRITE ALL THEIR OWN SONGS, TOO — WITH A LITTLE HELP FROM SOME OF THEIR FAMOUS FRIENDS, OF COURSE.

JOEL AND BENJI MADDEN OF GOOD CHARLOTTE. JOEL AND BENJI HELPED WRITE A FEW TRACKS WITH 5SOS IN 2003.

KAISER CHIEFS DRUMMER AND PRINCIPAL SONGWRITER, NICK HODGSON. HE HAS COLLABORATED WITH 5SOS.

In 2012, 5SOS checked off yet another one of their dream ambitions. They signed a publishing deal with Sony ATV. This momentous achievement gave the band the confidence to continue writing their own songs — an element close to the heart for them all, because they want to express their own experiences in their songs, not anybody else's — as they had done together in Michael's parents' house right from the start. After the publishing deal was signed, the boys started developing their ideas with other writers, such as Lo Russo and Joel Chapman of Australian band — and massive influence on 5SOS — Amy Meredith. Writing songs for their EPs *Somewhere New* and *Unplugged* gave the band the passion to put pen to paper and to tell their story from their own perspectivde as well as bring into sharp focus the type of songs they actually wanted to write. "The writing process is one of the best bits for us," Ashton remarked soon after signing the deal. "We all are songwriters and it's an awesome feeling to produce something as a band … and make some epic songs for our fans!"

With their debut album complete, the boys are able to look back at the unique writing and recording process with special memories. "I've written with all my heroes now," Luke exclaimed with wide-eyed disbelief. "I don't have any more heroes that I want to work with, except maybe Dave Grohl. I'd love to work with Dave Grohl." The album's writing and recording

process has seen the band hook up with many varied and successful performers and producers. "We've written with Benji and Joel from Good Charlotte," said Ashton. "We're big McFly fans, too. Luke and Michael wrote with Tom Fletcher and Dougie Payne and we wrote with James from Busted, too. It was a really good experience for us, working and writing with all these amazing people. They really make you up your game and adapt and learn." And while these super songwriters were brought in to help the band compose and structure their songs, the band was eager to make sure the songs they recorded for their debut album had their own 5SOS style and personality. "Even though we've written with a lot of amazing writers, we all had to remember that we're individuals, too and they don't have what we have," Luke said while applying the finishing touches to the album. "We brought our own special flavors to these writing sessions." With the album's release in 2014 — and 5SOS ready to burn even brighter than they do now — Michael is fairly simplistic about the whole writing experience. "We don't really mind what people think of us as long as they know we write our own stuff and play our own instruments."

With over 100 songs written for the debut album, the group should have enough material to please the 5SOS family for years to come. But being an ambitious bunch of boys, they will no doubt now start writing number one songs in their sleep!

MCBUSTED (TOM FLETCHER, DANNY JONES, DOUGIE POYNTER, HARRY JUDD, JAMES BOURNE, AND MATT WILLIS) BRINGS TOGETHER TWO SETS OF 5SOS'S MUSICAL HEROES.

YOUR NEW FAVORITE BAND: THE SUMMER LIGHTS BURN BRIGHT AT THE RITZ, MANCHESTER, FEBRUARY 25, 2014.

FIVE FRIENDS

WHEN 5SOS GOT THE CALL FROM ONE DIRECTION TO GO OUT ON THE ROAD WITH THEM ON THEIR MEGA-SIZED TAKE ME HOME TOUR IN 2013, THE GUYS WERE SPEECHLESS. BUT AS WE ALL NOW KNOW, THIS WAS JUST THE BEGINNING OF A BEAUTIFUL FRIENDSHIP ... AND MAYBE EVEN A FUTURE COLLABORATION?

"We were on our own tour in Adelaide at the time," Ashton recalls, describing the time they got the call that changed their lives. "We found out that Louis had found out about us on YouTube and we were like "WHOA! We were just a tiny, tiny band from Sydney and he tweeted about us ... and then it all just blossomed from there very quickly. It took us a while to decide what we wanted to do and if it was the right thing to do ... and it definitely was!" Ashton says of the historic moment: "Learning how to tour from the 1D lads really changed our lives." Calum agrees, "I still can't believe it happened."

Hilariously, the first time 5SOS met 1D, it didn't quite go as famously as both bands would have liked. "It all started with an awkward gathering at their house," Calum reported afterward. "1D speak really fast when they're together and we'd only ever met two Englishmen before them ... and we all just sat listening to them speak to each other. We needed subtitles! And because we speak quickly when we're together, it was just like a lot of people speaking gibberish in this one room! We couldn't understand them and they couldn't understand us. So, we just ate a lot of pizza — that's how we bonded."

In 2014, McFly and Busted formed a supergroup called McBusted. It makes you think. What would the possible 5SOS and One Direction collaboration be called? 5SOS1D? One Second of Direction? Whatever it would be called, having those nine boys write and record a song would be a definite global number one. "Who knows! It could happen," Michael said secretively. *Let's make it happen!*

ONE DIRECTION GAVE 5SOS A BOOST INTO THE BIG LEAGUE WHEN THEY ASKED THE NEW BAND TO SUPPORT THEM ON THEIR TWO WORLD TOURS.

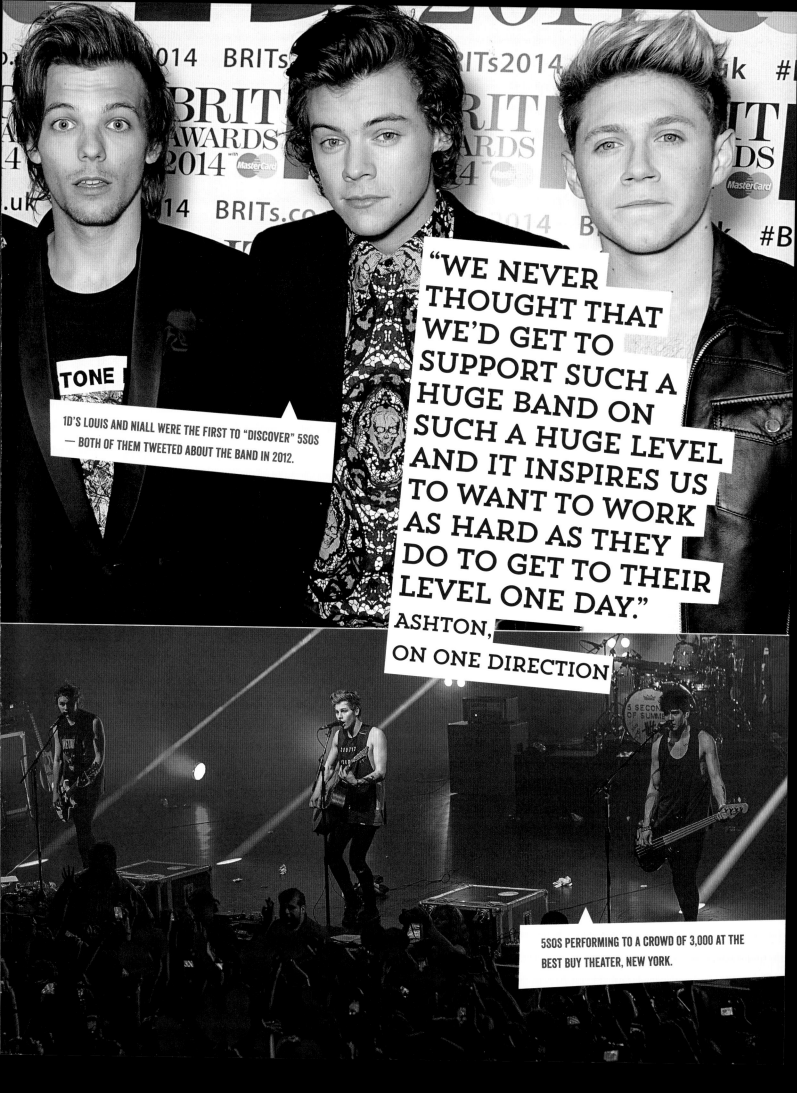

1D'S LOUIS AND NIALL WERE THE FIRST TO "DISCOVER" 5SOS — BOTH OF THEM TWEETED ABOUT THE BAND IN 2012.

"WE NEVER THOUGHT THAT WE'D GET TO SUPPORT SUCH A HUGE BAND ON SUCH A HUGE LEVEL. AND IT INSPIRES US TO WANT TO WORK AS HARD AS THEY DO TO GET TO THEIR LEVEL ONE DAY."
ASHTON, ON ONE DIRECTION

5SOS PERFORMING TO A CROWD OF 3,000 AT THE BEST BUY THEATER, NEW YORK.

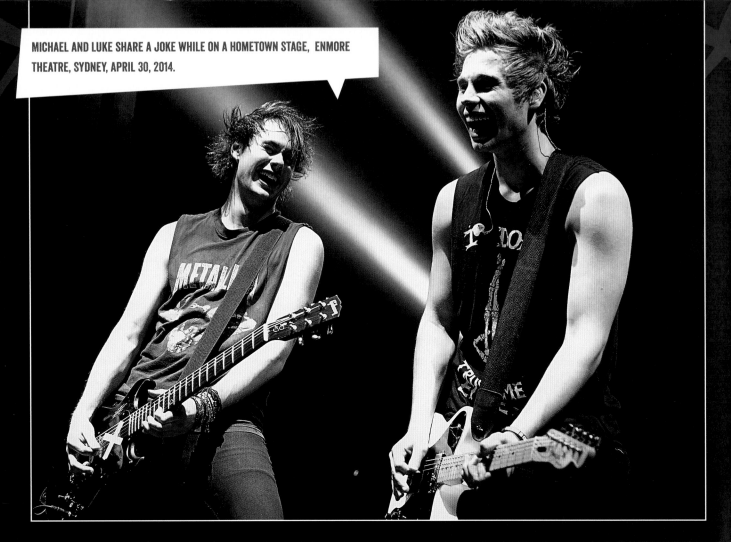

BOYS ON TOUR! ✕

NEW YORK. LOS ANGELES. SYDNEY. MADRID. PARIS. STOCKHOLM. LONDON. 5SOS
HAVE ALMOST BEEN AROUND THE WORLD! WITH MICHAEL AND CALUM NEVER
HAVING LEFT AUSTRALIA BEFORE THE BAND STARTED, IT'S FAIR TO SAY THAT
THEIR PASSPORTS NOW MUST HAVE MORE STAMPS THAN THEY EVER DREAMED
IMAGINABLE. AND THEY'VE ONLY JUST STARTED.

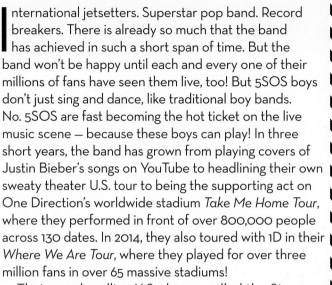

International jetsetters. Superstar pop band. Record breakers. There is already so much that the band has achieved in such a short span of time. But the band won't be happy until each and every one of their millions of fans have seen them live, too! But 5SOS boys don't just sing and dance, like traditional boy bands. No. 5SOS are fast becoming the hot ticket on the live music scene — because these boys can play! In three short years, the band has grown from playing covers of Justin Bieber's songs on YouTube to headlining their own sweaty theater U.S. tour to being the supporting act on One Direction's worldwide stadium *Take Me Home Tour*, where they performed in front of over 800,000 people across 130 dates. In 2014, they also toured with 1D in their *Where We Are Tour*, where they played for over three million fans in over 65 massive stadiums!

Their own headline U.S. show — called the *Stars, Stripes and Maple Syrup Tour* — sold out in an incredible three minutes. The band couldn't believe that America had embraced them so early on — unimaginable only 12 months earlier. "Obviously we saw a load of fans when we did the 1D tour in America," Ashton exclaimed, recalling their important gigs in New York, Los Angeles, Dallas, and San Francisco, "but it was really fun to see a lot of our own 5SOS fans who knew every word to our songs."

Over in Europe, at the start of 2014, the gang played to five countries in five days! This mini-tour saw them experience fan-frenzied chaos in France, Germany, Spain, and Sweden. They even had fans run after them down the street and line up outside the venues in the hopes that they would see their new favorite band for a split second. As always though, the band took the time to sign autographs and take dozens of selfies with their fans.

USA

"WHEN WE STARTED, I JUST ASSUMED THE USA WAS OUT OF REACH. WHEN YOU START A BAND YOU KIND OF JUST DO IT FOR FUN. YOU CAN NEVER EXPECT WHAT'S GOING TO HAPPEN, SO WHEN SUCCESS DOES HAPPEN, IT'S JUST AMAZING." MICHAEL

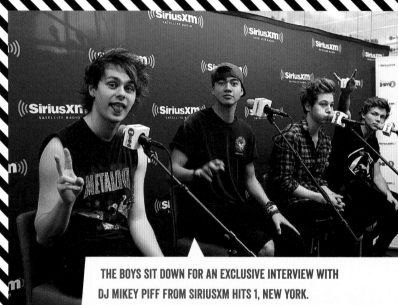

THE BOYS SIT DOWN FOR AN EXCLUSIVE INTERVIEW WITH DJ MIKEY PIFF FROM SIRIUSXM HITS 1, NEW YORK.

FRANCE & GERMANY

"WITH THE 5SOS LIVE EXPERIENCE YOU SHOULD EXPECT A ROCK SHOW, GUITAR SOLOS, AND HIGH ENERGY! WE LOVE MAKING A CROWD MOVE AND CREATING BIG ENERGY THROUGHOUT THE SHOW AND WE HOPE TO LEAVE AN IMPRESSION SO YOU LEAVE WANTING MORE!" LUKE

A HOMEMADE FAN POSTER OUTSIDE NRJ RADIO STATION, PARIS, 2014.

THE BOYS IN FRONT OF THEIR GROWING FANBASE IN PARIS AT LA GAIETE LYRIQUE, APRIL 4, 2014.

STOCKHOLM, SWEDEN IS TREATED TO A FRESH BATCH OF 5SOS SONGS WHILE THE BAND WERE TOURING THEIR *5 COUNTRIES 5 DAYS* SHOW, MARCH 2014.

HUNDREDS OF FANS CHANT "5SOS," AS THEY WAIT FOR THE BAND TO ARRIVE IN MILAN, ITALY, APRIL 3, 2014.

MADRID

"WE WORK A LOT ON SOCIAL MEDIA BECAUSE THAT'S WHERE WE STARTED REALLY, BUT IT'S JUST SO GOOD TO SEE THE FANS ON TOUR. THEY DO SO MUCH FOR US AND IT'S AMAZING." CALUM

UK

"[PLAYING IN THE UK] HAS BEEN SWEATY AND IT'S BEEN A PARTY! THE FANS HAVE BEEN AMAZING. IT'S ALSO BEEN FULL OF CHICKEN. WE'VE HAD A LOT OF NANDO'S WHILE ON TOUR IN THE UK! NANDOS – SHOW – THEN MORE CHICKEN AFTER THE SHOW, USUALLY A NANDO'S AGAIN."

AT THE SHEPHERDS BUSH EMPIRE, LONDON, MARCH 2014.

ASHTON KEEPS THE RHYTHM ON POINT.

AUSTRALIA

"AUSTRALIA WILL ALWAYS BE HOME FOR US BUT WE DON'T GET TO GO HOME THAT MUCH BECAUSE IT'S SO FAR AWAY!"
ASHTON

AT THE AUSTRALIAN HOMECOMING SHOW, THE BOYS WERE TREATED LIKE RETURNING HEROES!

CRAZY IN LOVE

"I THINK THE THREE BEST THINGS ABOUT BEING IN 5SOS IS BEING WITH YOUR BEST FRIENDS THAT YOU GREW UP WITH, DOING THE THING YOU LOVE AND MEETING ALL THE FANS." CALUM

"I LIKE TO THINK IT'S TRUE LOVE," MICHAEL ONCE SAID OF THEIR FANS. IT IS, BUT THE FANS' LOVE OF THEIR NEW FAVORITE BAND IS QUICKLY RECIPROCATED BY THE BOYS, WHO ALSO CAN'T QUITE BELIEVE THEIR LUCK.

Crazy. Insane. Amazing. These are words that are often, daily, used by the band to describe not only their fans, but what it's like to just have fans in the first place!

"We love you so much — thank you for making our dreams come true every day!" said Ashton in a recent interview. These gushings of love toward their fans have been everyday occurrences since the band had 12 people turn up to their first gig. And not a day goes by when at least one of the band members, if not all of them, proudly shout from the rooftops, or tweet in capital letters on Twitter: "WE HAVE THE BEST FANS IN THE WORLD!"

While fans all around the world have fallen in love with their new favorite band, the band themselves have found themselves falling in love with their

BRIGHT LIGHTS OF PHILLY: 5SOS'S SOLD-OUT CONCERT AT THE TOWER THEATER, PHILADELPHIA, APRIL 24, 2014. THE SHOW WAS PART OF THEIR STARS, STRIPES AND MAPLE SYRUP TOUR.

FANS WAIT FOR THEIR HEROES IN MILAN, APRIL 3, 2014.

ITALY

FREE HUGS for 5 SECONDS OF SUMMER MILANO

LOVE YU

HI HEY

SLSP

CAL LIENAD ASH MIKE

absolutely crazy but incredibly devoted fans, too. It's a two-way thing!

"It's crazy for us, but we're so grateful for every single person that supports us, not many people where we live get this kind of opportunity to do what they love," said Calum. Ashton agrees with his bandmate: "It's pretty insane to have that momentum and have people really love what you do." One Direction have their Directioneers, and Justin Bieber has his Beliebers, and even 5SOS's favorite band, Blink 182, had fans who called themselves 182ers. So that just leaves the question — what do fans of 5 Seconds of Summer call themselves? Seconders? Summerites? Fivers? At the moment, there isn't an exact answer to this question. Time will tell, the bigger, and more famous, the band get. "We call them 5SOSfans," Luke said, "but they can really call themselves whatever they want!" Whatever they end up being named, 5SOS fans are crazy in love with their new favorite band.

THOUSANDS OF FANS SING ALONG AS 5SOS PERFORM ONSTAGE AT THE PALAIS THEATRE, MELBOURNE, AUSTRALIA, MAY 3, 2014.

AT THEIR VERY FIRST BRIT AWARDS, O2 ARENA, LONDON ON FEBRUARY 19, 2014.
5SOS WERE MOBBED BY FANS ON THE RED CARPET.

HIGH FIVE ♥

BEING IN A SUCCESSFUL BAND WHERE YOUR MOST FAMOUS FANS ARE
THE BIGGEST BAND IN THE WORLD — ONE DIRECTION — AND WAKING
UP EVERY MORNING TO THE SCREAMS OF EXCITED FANS OUTSIDE YOUR
HOTEL ROOM MUST BE SURREAL? NOT FOR 5SOS, THEY'RE TAKING ALL
THE CRAZINESS OF SUPER-FAME, AND RECORD-BREAKING SUCCESS IN
STRIDE — BUT IT HELPS HAVING YOUR BEST FRIENDS BY YOUR SIDE.

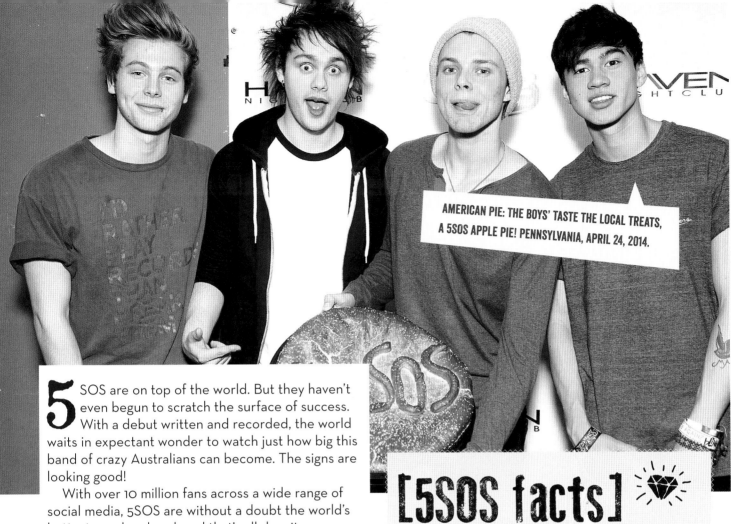

AMERICAN PIE: THE BOYS' TASTE THE LOCAL TREATS, A 5SOS APPLE PIE! PENNSYLVANIA, APRIL 24, 2014.

5SOS are on top of the world. But they haven't even begun to scratch the surface of success. With a debut written and recorded, the world waits in expectant wonder to watch just how big this band of crazy Australians can become. The signs are looking good!

With over 10 million fans across a wide range of social media, 5SOS are without a doubt the world's hottest new boy band, and that's all despite no promotion or publicity from any major record label.

Before the band get too big to measure, let's take a look at 5SOS's five greatest chart-topping moments so far...

[5SOS facts]

On April 9, 2014, the *She Looks So Perfect* EP debuted at number 2 on the *Billboard* 200. 5SOS have — and this is official — broken America before even releasing their debut album!

The band's first music release, an EP, called *Unplugged*, reached number 3 on the iTunes chart in Australia, and the Top 20 in both New Zealand and Sweden.

The music video for their first single "Out of My Limit," released on November 19, 2012, received over 100,000 views ... within the first 24 hours; It now has over 5 million views ... and rising!

The band's first major label single, "She Looks So Perfect" went to number 1 in 39 countries within two days of being released!

In March 2014, the band became only the fourth Australian band to reach the number 1 spot in the U.K. charts!

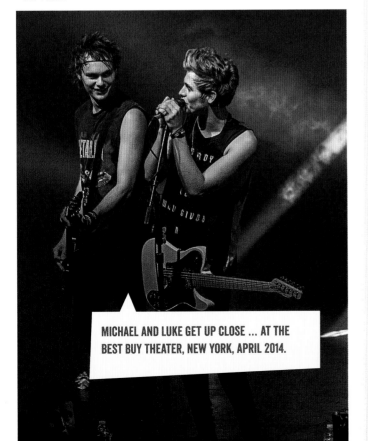

MICHAEL AND LUKE GET UP CLOSE ... AT THE BEST BUY THEATER, NEW YORK, APRIL 2014.

TOTAL CONTROL

//

DESPITE SIGNING A PUBLISHING DEAL IN 2012 THE GANG REMAIN AN INDEPENDENT ENTITY. THEY WERE DESPERATE TO RETAIN TOTAL CREATIVE CONTROL OF THEIR MUSIC AND TO CONTINUE RUNNING THE SHOW THEY HAD WORKED SO HARD TO BUILD UP. ON NOVEMBER 21, 2013, THE GOOD NEWS THE FANS HAD BEEN WAITING FOR FINALLY ARRIVED: 5SOS HAD SIGNED A RECORD DEAL — AND CREATED THEIR OWN LABEL, TOO!

AN ACOUSTIC PERFORMANCE OF NEW MATERIAL AT THE Q102 IN PENNSYLVANIA ON APRIL 24, 2014.

For the millions of fans desperate to buy as many 5SOS songs as they could, the fact that they couldn't was becoming a growing, alarming mystery. Although the band had formed in 2011, by early 2014 they had yet to release their debut album . This situation is also unheard of in today's make-a-quick-buck music industry. Well, that's another reason 5SOS are so different. After spending three years building a large fanbase, with no promotion or publicity by any major recording label, they took their time selecting the right record label. The band have so much hype and buzz surrounding them that when they do release their album — and announce their own tour — they are bound to sell out in, well, five seconds!

In a newsletter on their website — www.5sos.com — the band posted this notice: "We also have some AMAZING news, which is really exciting for us boys — we've signed to Capitol Records!"

But that wasn't *all* the good news. Not only did the band sign to a major record label, they also announced the launch of their own one, too, called Hi Or Hey Records.

Taking being unique to a whole new level, 5SOS's new record label, Hi Or Hey Records, will be a loving home for upcoming future artists. The label also shows just how serious the band takes its music and its fans. "Hi Or Hey Records means we can stay in control of our career. Things have gone pretty well with you and us running the show. We want to keep it that way." We couldn't agree more, could we?

Finally, after teasing their fans for three long years, the band announced the release date of its debut album for June 30, 2014, mere days before the U.K. leg of their HUGE Wembley Stadium shows with 1D. The news came from the band's website in late May, with a quick note from the boys: "We're soooo excited to finally be releasing our debut album." Fans are treated to newly recorded versions of older tracks, such as "Heartbreak Girl," as well as nine new and previously unreleased songs, including the song of summer 2014, "She Looked So Perfect."

THE BAND MAY FOOL AROUND AND GOOF WITH EACH OTHER ONSTAGE, BUT THEY'RE NOTHING BUT SERIOUS WHEN IT COMES TO THEIR MUSIC.

"WE'RE TRULY THE LUCKIEST TEENAGERS IN THE WORLD TO HAVE YOU." 5SOS

REHEARSING AT THE FRENCH RADIO STATION NRJ ON APRIL 2, 2014, PARIS. THEY SPENT JUST 24 HOURS IN FRANCE BEFORE FLYING TO ITALY!

SONG OF THE SUMMER ✕

AFTER SIGNING THEIR LANDMARK RECORD DEAL, 5SOS SPENT THREE MONTHS RECORDING THEIR DEBUT MAJOR LABEL SINGLE. IT BECAME THEIR FIRST WORLDWIDE NUMBER 1 SMASH HIT. DESCRIBED BY MOST MUSIC JOURNALISTS AS "THE SONG OF THE SUMMER 2014," "SHE LOOKS SO PERFECT" ROSE LIKE THE SUN TO THE HIGHEST POINT ON THE CHARTS ... EVERYWHERE!

"I actually cried when I found out," Ashton said about the band's incredible Number 1 success, not only in their home country, but in 39 other countries around the globe! "I can't believe how we have all come together, you guys (5SOS family and fans) are the single reason this has all happened, I love you all so much, we are so proud of you."

"She Looks So Perfect" was one of just scores of songs written during the summer of 2013, when the band lived together in L.A. (and London). Those of you who have seen the band's Twitter and Instagram videos will know how much fun this was for the band! They also spent time in writing sessions with various producers, songwriters, and best-selling artists.

MEETING AND GREETING THEIR BRITISH FANS IN GLASGOW, MARCH 24, 2014.

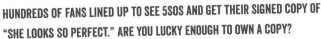

"We wrote 'She Looks So Perfect' with our friend Jake Sinclair in L.A. He came to us with the idea of the chorus, which talks about standing around in underwear! He said 'bear with me, I know it's kind of weird,' but we told him we didn't mind because we love weird lyrics. I think the song stands out from anything else that's out there at the moment," Luke announced proudly while on duty promoting the single in February 2014. Calum agreed: "The song's about having a person next to you wearing clothes after you've woken up, or whatever, and there's something really sweet about it. The funny thing is we all think that American Apparel underwear is really ugly!" And that's coming from Calum who is renowned for his embarrassing underwear!

To coincide with the start of the band's tour with One Direction in June 2014, the boys released their EP *Don't Stop* in four different formats, with the new tracks "Rejects," "Try Hard," "If You Don't Know," and "Wrapped Around Your Finger."

A PROUD MOMENT IN ANY BAND'S CAREER — HOLDING YOUR FIRST EVER SINGLE. "SHE LOOKS SO PERFECT" WAS A WORLDWIDE SMASH IN 2014.

CREDITS/ACKNOWLEDGMENTS

//

SOURCES

p4 quote from www.seventeen.com interview with Kristin Harris
p6 quote from Summer Chart Show interview with Stephanie Faleo, and from 5SOS's YouTube Channel
p8 quotes from www.popscoop.org interview with Isaac Marc-Tressler and Summer Chart Show interview with Stephanie Faleo,
p10 quotes from 5SOS's YouTube Channel and Summer Chart Show interview with Stephanie Faleo, www.popscoop.org interview with Isaac Marc-Tressler, and Kidd Nation TV interview with Trey Peart
p12 quotes from www.seventeen.com interview with Kristin Harris and 5SOS's YouTube Channel, Summer Chart Show interview with Stephanie Faleo, www.popscoop.org interview with Isaac Marc-Tressler, interview on Kidd Nation TV with Trey Peart, and www.seventeen.com interview with Kristin Harris
p15 quote from interview www.hmv.com with Tom, editor
p16, School's Out quote from Norwest Christian College website bio
p18, Under the Influence quote from interview www.hmv.com with Tom, editor
p20, Rock On quote from www.seventeen.com interview with Kristin Harris
p22, Take Off quote from Sunrise interview with Natalie Barr
p26, No Limits quotes from www.popscoop.org interview with Isaac Marc-Tressler, The Showbiz411 interview with Laurie Blake, and www.theaureview.com interview with Sosefina Fuamoli
p34, Boys on Tour quote from www.theaureview.com interview with Sosefina Fuamoli
p36, Boys On Tour quote from www.theaureview.com interview with Sosefina Fuamoli
p37 Calum quote from www.fuse.tv interview with Jeff Benjamin
p38 quote from www.popscoop.org interview with Isaac Marc-Tressler
p40 quote from www.seventeen.com interview with Kristin Harris
p41 quote from Kidd Nation TV interview with Trey Peart
p44, Total Control quote from http://5sos-official.tumblr.com/hiorheyrecords
p46, Song of the Summer quote from www.dailymail.co.uk
p47 quote from interview with the band on www.mtv.com

GENERAL SOURCES

5SOS Live Stream on their own Google Hangout
Interview with Smallsy from NOVA FM.
Interview with the band on BBC Radio 1 (the band were in their pants)

PICTURE CREDITS

The publishers would like to thank the following sources for their kind permission to reproduce the pictures in this book.

Key
t = top, b = bottom, l = left, r = right

Page 4 Splash News/Corbis; 5 MediaPunch/Rex Features; 6 Norwest Christian College, New South Wales, Australia; 7l C Brandon/Getty Images; 7r Splash News/Corbis; 8tl Splash News/Corbis; 8tr Norwest Christian College, New South Wales, Australia; 8b Michael Hurcomb/Corbis; 9 D Dipasupil/Getty Images; 10 AGF s.r.l/Rex Features; 11t MediaPunch/Rex Features; 11bl Splash News/Corbis; 11br Myrna Suarez/Getty Images; 12 Splash News/Corbis; 13l Graham Denholm/Getty Images; 13tr David Wolff-Patrick/Getty Images; 13br Mark Metcalfe/Getty Images; 14 Brianne Makin/Newspix/Rex Features; 15t Myrna Suarez/Getty Images; 15b Noel Kessel/Newspix/Rex Features; 16 Norwest Christian College, New South Wales, Australia; 17t Sharkywoo/Wikimedia Commons; 17b Norwest Christian College, New South Wales, Australia; 18l Tim Mosenfelder/Getty Images; 18r Nigel Crane/Getty Images; 19t Brendon Thorne/Getty Images; 19b Myrna Suarez/Getty Images; 20t J. Shearer/Getty Images; 20bl Michael Ochs Archives/Getty Images; 20br Joe Giron/Corbis; 21 Bob King/Corbis; 22t AKM-GSI/Splash News/Corbis; 22b D Dipasupil/Getty Images; 23t Myrna Suarez/Getty Images; 23b Mark Metcalfe/Getty Images; 24-25 Brianne Makin/Newspix/Rex Features; 26t Graham Denholm/Getty Images; 26b AKM-GSI/Splash News/Corbis; 27 Justin Lloyd/Newspix/Rex Features; 28 Michael Hurcomb/Corbis; 29tl NBC/Getty Images; 29tr Laszlo Beliczay/epa/Corbis; 29b Dave J Hogan/Getty Images; 30-31 Andrew Benge/Getty Images; 32 FOX Image Collection/Getty Images; 33t David M. Benett/Getty Images; 33b Myrna Suarez/Getty Images; 34 Mark Metcalfe/Getty Images; 35t Robin Marchant/Getty Images; 35b Scott Legato/Getty Images; 36t Marc Piasecki/Getty Images; 36b David Wolff-Patrick/Getty Images; 37t IBL/Rex Features; 37b AGF s.r.l/Rex Features; 38t C Brandon/Getty Images; 38b C Brandon/Getty Images; 39t John Grainger/Newspix/Rex Features; 39b Justin Lloyd/Newspix/Rex Features; 40t John Lamparski/Getty Images; 40b Owen Sweeney/Invision/Press Association Images; 41t Justin Lloyd/Newspix/Rex Features; 41b Splash News/Corbis; 42 David M. Benett/Getty Images; 43t MediaPunch/Rex Features; 43b Myrna Suarez/Getty Images; 44 Bill McCay/Getty Images; 45t D Dipasupil/Getty Images; 45b David Wolff-Patrick/Getty Images; 46 Mirrorpix; 47t Splash News/Corbis; 47b Splash News/Corbis; 48 Mark Metcalfe/Getty Images; Poster Larry Busacca/Getty Images.

Every effort has been made to acknowledge correctly and contact the source and/or copyright holder of each picture and Carlton Books Limited apologizes for any unintentional errors or omissions, which will be, corrected in future editions of this book.